LeBron James

By Rachel Stuckey

Crabtree Publishing Company

www.crabtreebooks.com

Crabtree Publishing Company

www.crabtreebooks.com

Author: Rachel Stuckey
Publishing plan research and development:
Sean Charlebois, Reagan Miller
Crabtree Publishing Company
Coordinating editor: Laura Durman
Editors: Clare Hibbert, Kathy Middleton,
Jessica Shapiro
Proofreader: Kelly McNiven
Photo researcher: Clare Hibbert
Series and cover design: Ken Wright
Layout: sprout.uk.com
**Production coordinator and
prepress technician:** Ken Wright
Print coordinators: Katherine Berti,
Margaret Amy Salter

Photographs:
Alamy: © AF Archive: pages 6, 7; © Aflo Co.
Ltd.: page 24; © Boitano Photography: page
28; © ZUMA Press, Inc.: page 25; © ZUMA
Wire Service: pages 12, 13, 15
Corbis: © Michael J. Le Brecht II / NewSport:
page 8; © Richard C. Lewis / Icon SMI:
page 22; © Rhona Wise / Icon SMI: page 21
Getty Images: pages 5, 23; © MCT: page 17;
© Sports Illustrated: page 9
Keystone Press: Zumapress.com: cover
Photoshot: © Everett: page 10
Rex Features: © Startraks Photo: page 27
Shutterstock.com: © Sam Aranov: page 26;
© Songquan Deng: page 19; © Domenic
Gareri: pages 1, 18, 20; © Scott Meivogel:
page 11
Wikimedia Commons: © Keith Allison:
pages 4, 14; © Richard Giles: page 16

Produced for Crabtree Publishing Company by
Discovery Books

Library and Archives Canada Cataloguing in Publication

Stuckey, Rachel
      Lebron James / Rachel Stuckey.

(Superstars!)
Includes index.
Issued also in electronic formats.
ISBN 978-0-7787-1047-9 (bound).--ISBN 978-0-7787-1052-3 (pbk.)

      1. James, LeBron--Juvenile literature. 2. Basketball players--
United States--Biography--Juvenile literature. I. Title.
II. Series: Superstars! (St. Catharines, Ont.)

GV884.J36S78 2013   j796.323092   C2013-900434-3

Library of Congress Cataloging-in-Publication Data

Stuckey, Rachel.
      Lebron James / by Rachel Stuckey.
         pages cm. -- (Superstars!)
      Includes index.
      ISBN 978-0-7787-1047-9 (reinforced library binding) --
ISBN 978-0-7787-1052-3 (pbk.) -- ISBN 978-1-4271-9298-1
(electronic pdf) -- ISBN 978-1-4271-9222-6 (electronic html)
      1. James, LeBron--Juvenile literature. 2. Basketball players--United
States--Biography--Juvenile literature. 3. African American
basketball players--Biography--Juvenile literature. I. Title.

GV884.J36S88 2013
796.323092--dc23
[B]
                                                            2013001649

Crabtree Publishing Company

www.crabtreebooks.com   1-800-387-7650

Printed in the USA/052013/JA20130412

Published in Canada
Crabtree Publishing
616 Welland Ave.
St. Catharines, ON
L2M 5V6

Published in the United States
Crabtree Publishing
PMB 59051
350 Fifth Avenue, 59th Floor
New York, New York 10118

Published in the United Kingdom
Crabtree Publishing
Maritime House
Basin Road North, Hove
BN41 1WR

Published in Australia
Crabtree Publishing
3 Charles Street
Coburg North
VIC, 3058

CONTENTS

Words that are defined in the glossary are in
bold type the first time they appear in the text.

Meet LeBron

LeBron Raymone James is one of the best basketball players in the world. Some say he is the best player in history, and he has only been playing in the National Basketball Association (NBA) for nine seasons. Declared NBA **Rookie** of the Year in 2004, LeBron has gone on to become an eight-time NBA All-Star and a two-time Olympic gold medalist.

When he played for the Cavaliers, LeBron wore #23—the same number as his hero, Michael Jordan.

INSPIRATION

As a kid, LeBron worshipped Michael Jordan and had posters of him all over his room. He never imagined that one day they would be friends!

Early Life

LeBron had a difficult childhood growing up in Akron, Ohio. His teenaged mother, Gloria James, raised him on her own. Gloria struggled to make ends meet and battled personal problems after the death of her mother. She and LeBron were forced to move from apartment to apartment as she bounced between jobs. Despite her struggles, Gloria was a loving mother who worked hard to keep her son clothed and fed. However, having an unsettled home life made it difficult for LeBron to make friends.

Sports was always where LeBron excelled, and he formed a strong bond with his football coach, Frankie Walker. However, he found it increasingly hard to concentrate on his studies at school. By the fourth grade. LeBron had practically stopped attending altogether.

LeBron's proud mother Gloria holds a picture of her son as she cheers him on during a high school game.

Stepping In

Noticing his poor attendance, Frankie spoke to LeBron's mother about it. Gloria agreed that LeBron needed a more stable home environment and allowed her son to move in with the Walker family. The newfound stability was just what Lebron needed. He went back to school and, in the fifth grade, won the school attendance record. When he eventually returned to live with Gloria 18 months later, the Walkers continued to help and support them both.

He Said It

[I] lived in the projects…You hear a lot of police sirens, you hear a lot of gunfire…But sports carried me away from being in a gang, or being associated with drugs. Sports was my way out.
—LeBron James, interview with Larry King, June 2010

Terrific Teammates

Through Frankie's sons, LeBron met four young basketball players: Sian Cotton, Dru Joyce III, Willie McGee, and Romeo Travis. They formed a team, gathering at a local community center to be put through their paces by Keith Dambrot—the former head coach at Central Michigan University. Together they developed a tremendous **camaraderie** and sixth sense for the game.

The friends drew national attention in 1997 when they qualified for the Under/6th Grade AAU (Amateur Athletic Union) National Championships in Salt Lake City, Utah. Two years later, they made it to the AAU Under/8th Grade final in Orlando, Florida. Although they lost the game, the six-foot-tall LeBron was already being recognized for his incredible playing skills.

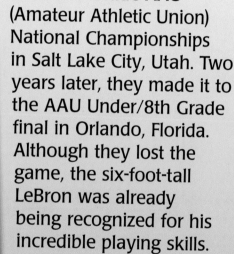

LeBron (second from right) raises his trophy to celebrate a grade school win.

He Said It

I think we all were taught the game, and we had a good understanding of the game even before we got to high school. . . . that's why we did so well as a unit. We were all on the same page . . . and we were ready to compete.

—Willie McGee, in an interview with HollywoodChicago.com, October 2009

The story of the Akron Fab Five is told in the 2008 **documentary** *More Than a Game*. Taking a moment to pose during filming are, from left to right, Sian Cotton, LeBron James, Dru Joyce III, Romeo Travis, and Willie McGee.

St. Vincent-St. Mary

The African-American kids in LeBron's Akron neighborhood all went to the local public school. But LeBron and his friends chose to attend St. Vincent-St. Mary High School (STVM), a mostly white Catholic school. It was a tough decision for them but STVM had a great basketball team. The choice was not popular in his community, but LeBron never regretted it.

The Akron Fab Five

By now, LeBron and his teammates were known as the Akron Fab Five. As students at STVM, they won many tournaments, including state and national championships. Today, these high school teammates are still LeBron's closest friends.

A Star is Born!

LeBron became a superstar in high school. During his freshman year he was a starter on the basketball team, and the team won the state championship. As a sophomore, he was named Ohio's Mr. Basketball by the Ohio High School Basketball Coaches Association.

LeBron plays a home game for STVM in 2001, during his sophomore year. Due to the intense interest surrounding him, the game was played at the University of Akron, which offered a larger seating capacity.

In the same year, LeBron attended the Adidas ABCD Camp for prominent high school players at Fairleigh-Dickinson University in New Jersey. The highlight was a showdown between LeBron and New York sensation Lenny Cooke. LeBron outscored Cooke 24–9. His remarkable talent was beginning to draw national attention.

He Said It

Thing is, he's a celebrity—small-scale for now, but probably not much longer. He just finished his sophomore season, and yet he might just be the best high school basketball player in America.
—Ryan Jones, sports writer, in *SLAM Magazine*, September 2001

NBA No No

LeBron was very eager to play in the NBA. He wanted to skip playing basketball in college and go straight to the pros. In fact, when Lebron was named Gatorade National Player of the Year in his junior year of high school, he asked the NBA to include him in the 2002 **draft**. However, the NBA denied his request—all draft picks must be high school graduates.

Though disappointed, LeBron turned the rejection into motivation to work even harder. He resolved to spend more time in the gym to improve his game. Televised by ESPN2, a staggering 1.67 million households tuned in to watch him play in STVM's December contest against Oak Hill. He rose to the occasion, posting 31 points and 13 rebounds.

KING JAMES

Since high school, LeBron's nickname has been "King James." But he never acted like a king—he has always worked hard and shared the ball. King James is a team player.

Sports Illustra

Winter Olympics

WHAT MAKES THESE GAMES SO SPECIAL

U.S. SNOWBOARDERS RULE THE HALFPIPE

THE CHOSEN ONE

High school junior
LeBron James
would be an NBA
lottery pick right now

FEBRUARY 18, 2002 www.cnnsi.com
AOL Keyword: Sports Illustrated

During his junior year, LeBron was featured on the cover of *Sports Illustrated*. The photo shoot took place at the STVM gym.

Networking

By now, interest in LeBron was reaching fever pitch. Parents asked him to pose for pictures with them at his high school games, and kids begged for autographs. The top sports shoe companies were battling for his attention, and NBA managers were turning up to watch him play. As well as hanging out with his favorite rapper, Jay-Z, and counting Boston Celtics star Antoine Walker as a friend, LeBron was asked to play in Michael Jordan's top-secret workouts in Chicago. The only schoolboy invited, LeBron relished this opportunity to train alongside—and hang out with—his hero.

Finding Love

Around this time, LeBron had started dating Savannah Brinson. A cheerleader and junior at a rival high school, Savannah had no idea who LeBron was when he first approached her. Having accepted an invitation to watch him play basketball, she quickly realized just how popular he was. The pair were soon inseparable. Brinson described him as a normal high school senior, despite his increasing level of fame.

LeBron and his high-school sweetheart, Savannah Brinson, pose with Jay-Z in 2007.

The Cleveland Cavaliers chose LeBron in the 2003 draft.

Already Number One

In the 2003 NBA draft, LeBron was the number one overall draft pick—in other words, he was picked first. He was selected by the Cleveland Cavaliers. Akron is only 40 miles (64 km) from Cleveland, so LeBron was not only the superstar rookie, but also a local hero!

Prep-to-Pro

At last, LeBron was a **prep-to-pro** player, a term given to players who go straight from high school to the NBA. Most players start their careers playing college basketball. It is uncommon for high school players to be drafted, and even less common for them to be the first player selected. Other famous prep-to-pro players are Kevin Garnett and Kobe Bryant.

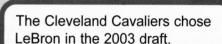

DRAFT CLASS

Chris Bosh and Dwyane Wade, who both now play for the Miami Heat, were also drafted in 2003—they are part of LeBron's "draft class." Chris was drafted fourth by the Toronto Raptors and Dwyane was drafted fifth by the Miami Heat.

11

Path to Stardom

LeBron wasted no time claiming his place in sports history. In his first NBA game he scored 25 points. At 19 years of age he became the youngest NBA player in history to score 40 points in a single game. He was also one of the only players to average at least 20 points a game in his rookie season. It's no wonder he was named Rookie of the Year!

LeBron drives against Speedy Claxton of the Warriors during his rookie season with the Cavaliers.

In Private

Unfortunately, Cleveland did not make the NBA **play-offs** that year. But LeBron had other things on his mind. He and Savannah were going to have a baby. At first she was concerned about the effect the news might have on LeBron's career. But the father-to-be reassured her. They would handle their family and his career together.

She Said It

I was very scared . . . But [LeBron] said, "It's not going to slow me down, and it's not going to slow you down. We're going to keep doing what we have to do. —Savannah Brinson, in an interview in *Harper's Bazaar,* August 9, 2010

International Basketball

In 2004, LeBron was chosen to be part of Team USA at the Athens Olympics. But it was a disappointing year for the United States basketball team, they only placed third. This was the first time since NBA players had been permitted to play in the Olympics that Team USA had not won gold.

LeBron was the youngest member of the squad. Despite the result, he relished the opportunity to take part, and to train and play with veterans Allen Iverson and Tim Duncan. He said that they—along with his impending fatherhood—inspired him to come back better the following season.

JUNIOR JOY

Just over a month after the 2004 Olympic games, on October 6, LeBron's son was born. The couple named the baby LeBron James Jr.

LeBron gets an easy dunk against Joaquim Gomes of Angola in a men's preliminary game at the 2004 Olympics.

He Said It

Sometimes in the past . . . [if] I thought I could have played better I would let it hang over my head for a long time . . . But now, being a parent . . . I forget about any mistake I ever made . . . [Parenthood] has made me grow as an individual and grow as a man.
—LeBron James, in *Seattle Post-Intelligencer*, December 10, 2005

The Second Season

CHALK CLAP

LeBron's **ritual** before every game is to clap his hands together and toss a cloud of chalk in the air. It's also something that his hero Michael Jordan used to do.

During his next season in 2004–2005, LeBron was voted to the All-Star team. He also became the youngest player in history to achieve a triple-double—when a player's points, rebounds, and assists are all in the "double digits." In one game, LeBron scored 56 points, a career best. Incredibly, the Cavaliers still didn't make the play-offs.

Third Time Around

In the 2005–2006 season, LeBron continued to impress. He played in the All-Star Game again, and helped his team win by scoring 29 points. The Cavaliers also made the play-offs for the first time since 1998. Despite an outstanding performance from LeBron, Cleveland lost to the Detroit Pistons in the second round.

Fans look on in delight as LeBron performs his pregame ritual.

Making Choices

After his third season, LeBron renewed his **contract** with the Cavaliers, but he took less money so that he could have a more flexible agreement. This gave him the option to change teams in three years.

In the Lead

Throughout the 2006–2007 season, LeBron continued to prove his worth, ranking as the team's leading scorer more often than not. He became one of only two players in NBA history to score an average of at least 27 points per game for three years in a row. The Cavaliers made it to the finals, but lost to the San Antonio Spurs. On the day of the final game, Savannah gave birth to their second son—Bryce Maximus.

The Cavaliers made it to the 2007 NBA finals, but lost to the San Antonio Spurs. Here Spurs player Tim Duncan tries to block a shot by LeBron.

During the following season, 23-year-old LeBron became the youngest player to score 10,000 points in the NBA. And he did it in only 368 games. This was LeBron's fifth season with Cleveland. The team made the play-offs but disappointed fans again, losing to the Boston Celtics in the second round.

Striving for Gold

Since the 2004 Olympics, Team USA had worked hard to prepare for the 2008 Games in Beijing, China. They qualified in 2007 by winning against Argentina in the **FIBA** Americas Championship final.

In their first Beijing game, Team USA beat the strong team from China, which included NBA superstar Yao Ming. They went on to reach the finals, playing against Spain in the gold medal game. There were four NBA players on the Spanish team, but the United States still won—118 to 107. Team USA had reclaimed Olympic gold.

Team USA teammates at the 2008 Olympic Games, from left: Dwayne Wade, Carmelo Anthony, LeBron, and Chris Bosh.

Defense, Defense

Back home with the Cavaliers, LeBron showed that he could do more than just score points. He came in second for the Defensive Player of the Year award. He also improved his **free throws**, making almost 8 out of every 10 shots. This sixth season was one of the team's best. LeBron was selected as the league's Most Valuable Player (MVP). The team fought hard in the play-offs but lost in the finals to the Orlando Magic.

Shaq Attack

In the 2009–2010 season, superstar Shaquille O'Neal joined the Cavaliers. LeBron had one year left on his contract. Shaq and LeBron worked closely together, but Shaq later described tensions within the team. He claimed LeBron received special treatment as an encouragement to stay

Teammates Shaquille O'Neal and LeBron argue an offensive foul during their 2010 quarterfinal game against the Chicago Bulls.

with Cleveland the following year. Unfortunately, the Cavaliers once again lost in the second round of play-offs. Many, including Shaq, blamed LeBron for not playing well in important games.

He Said It

There's no question in Game 5 LeBron was kind of out of it. I always believed he could turn it on at any moment, but for some reason he didn't.
—Shaquille O'Neal, in *Shaq Uncut: My Story*, 2011

A Change in Direction

In 2010, LeBron's contract with the Cavaliers ended and he became a **free agent**. He could decide which team he wanted to play for. Cleveland wanted him to stay and many other teams were after him, too. LeBron's goal was to join a team that could win the NBA championship.

Dwyane Wade welcomed two new teammates in 2010.

The Decision

LeBron was persuaded to make his announcement on a live television special on ESPN called *The Decision*. The money made from the TV show would be donated to the youth charity, Boys and Girls Clubs of America. On the show, after a lengthy interview, LeBron revealed his decision to sign with the Miami Heat so he could play with stars Dwyane Wade and newly-signed Chris Bosh.

Fall From Grace

Unfortunately for LeBron, the reaction to the TV show was harsh. Cleveland fans were mad that LeBron was quitting their team, and NBA fans thought he was being a show-off on television. Some players, even some of his idols, thought he should have chosen a team where he would be the only star. Overnight, LeBron became the most unpopular player in the NBA.

The American Airlines Arena in Miami, Florida, is home to the Miami Heat.

Responding to the Critics

At first, LeBron did not agree with the fans' and the media's opinion about *The Decision*. By joining Miami, he had fulfilled his dream to join a team where he wasn't the only star player. He was also happy to have been able to raise millions of dollars for the Boys and Girls Clubs. Eventually, LeBron did express regret about the way he made his announcement on TV. By then, critics were beginning to soften their attitude toward him, too.

He Said It

I love his game, his attitude and especially the way he has carried himself in the face of unparalleled hatred. . . . He hasn't pouted about his treatment. If anything, he has taken all the abuse and carried it nobly. . . . That takes strength.
—Rick Morrissey, sports writer, in the *Chicago Sun-Times*, July 13, 2012

Moving to Miami

On the day that LeBron signed his contract with the Heat, the team had a party to welcome their new players. An excited LeBron predicted that Miami would create a championship-winning **dynasty**. LeBron looked forward to settling into the Florida lifestyle. However, Savannah did not want to uproot her sons from their neighborhood in Ohio. With LeBron Jr. starting school, they decided to split the family's time between Miami and Akron.

LeBron plays against the Toronto Raptors during his first season with Miami.

Playing the Villain

In his first year with the Heat, LeBron wasn't popular with opposing basketball fans. The negative spirit of the fans forced LeBron into the role of villain in the NBA during the 2010–2011 season. He didn't like it.

He Said It

It basically turned me into somebody I wasn't. You start to hear "the villain," now you have to be the villain . . . I started to play . . . angry . . . and that's not the way I play the game of basketball.
—LeBron James, quoted in *USA Today*, December 6, 2011

First Season in Miami

Even though the fans booed him, LeBron still set new records in 2010–2011. By the end of the season he was ranked second in the league for average number of points scored. His teammate Dwyane Wade was also one of the league's top scorers. Together they scored more than 4,000 points!

SHE SAID YES

LeBron did have something to celebrate in 2011. He proposed to Savannah in front of his teammates and friends at a New Year's Eve celebration party. His high-school sweetheart said "yes." The couple plan to marry in 2013.

Finals Fail

Despite this success, LeBron's first year with Miami was a disappointment. The Heat lost to the Dallas Mavericks in the NBA Finals. LeBron's performance in the play-offs wasn't as good as usual. His scoring average during the finals was less than 18 points per game. Even LeBron said he felt he could have played better, but he just didn't have enough game-changing plays to turn games around.

LeBron stands for "The Star-Spangled Banner" before a game during his first season with Miami.

The 2011-2012 Season

LeBron started his second season with Miami determined to make a change. He wanted to return to the joy of playing. The Heat started off strong, and LeBron had another great season. In the All-Star Game, he scored 36 points and shot six 3-pointers, tying the All-Star Game record. And once again, LeBron was named the league's MVP.

Powering Through

In 2012, the Miami Heat played the Oklahoma City Thunder in the NBA Finals. In Game 4, LeBron had leg cramps and had to be carried off the court with only five minutes left in the game. Amazingly, LeBron recovered in time to score a three-pointer that helped Miami win.

LeBron takes a jump shot at the South Florida All-Star Classic on October 8, 2011.

NBA Championship

In Game 5, LeBron achieved a triple-double, with 26 points, 11 rebounds, and 13 assists. Miami won the game and the championship. The years of hard work had finally paid off. LeBron was also named the NBA Finals Most Valuable Player, silencing his critics and proving that his move to the Heat was the right decision.

Repeat Golds

LeBron helped Team USA to victory once again at the 2012 Olympic Games. He is one of only three players to win an Olympic gold medal and the NBA championship in the same year. Michael Jordan and Scottie Pippen are the other two.

LeBron celebrates with his partner Savannah and their two sons after the Heat wins Game 5 of the 2012 Finals.

He Said It

[Winning the championship] means everything. I made a difficult decision to leave Cleveland but I understood what my future was about . . . I knew we had a bright future [in Miami]. This is a dream come true for me. This is definitely when it pays off.
—LeBron James, quoted in the *Houston Chronicle*, June 22, 2012

Off the Court

The Public Figure

LeBron's gift for basketball has made him very wealthy. In addition to his NBA salary, he makes money from **endorsements** for companies including Nike, Sprite, Upper Deck, and McDonalds. One company, Fenway Sports Group, manages all of LeBron's **marketing** deals. Because of his deal with Fenway, LeBron now owns part of Liverpool F.C., a soccer team in the English Premier League. Being a sports superstar is big business!

The Liverpool soccer team line up before a match in December 2012.

He Said It

He's intelligent and remarkably mature, and beyond that, he's also extremely savvy about building and maintaining his own image.
—Phil Taylor, sports writer, in *Sports Illustrated*, June 2, 2009

Giving Back

Like many superstars, LeBron puts some of his money to good use. He is an active **philanthropist**. He is a big supporter of Boys and Girls Clubs of America, a charity that provides after-school and summer programs and activities to kids for free.

26 SECONDS CAMPAIGN

Every 26 seconds in the United States a student drops out of school. LeBron's foundation works closely with the State Farm insurance company's 26 Seconds campaign to change that statistic and encourage students to stay in school and graduate.

Staying in School

LeBron has also started his own charity, the LeBron James Family Foundation, in Akron, Ohio. It supports the Akron Public Schools' after-school program. The foundation raises money with its annual bike-a-thon in Akron. In 2011, the bike-a-thon became the Wheels for Education program. Each year, more than 300 third-grade students are given bikes and enter a nine-year program to help them stay in school.

LeBron's "I Promise" band is a reminder of the work his foundation does. Students promise to go to school, be respectful, be active, and make good decisions. In return LeBron—their hero—promises to be the best role model he can be.

A TV Star is Born

LeBron has a natural talent for performance. In 2007 he co-hosted the ESPY Awards with television personality Jimmy Kimmel. And in 2009 LeBron had a **cameo role** in the HBO comedy drama series *Entourage*.

Making Them Laugh

PERFECT PITCH

LeBron and rapper and director Ice Cube have **pitched** an idea to the ABC television network. They hope to make a one-hour special about LeBron's life.

LeBron also appeared in an episode of the sketch comedy show *Saturday Night Live*. He hosted the 2007 **season premiere** of the popular show. Lorne Michaels, the producer of *Saturday Night Live*, predicted that LeBron would do well because he has a good sense of humor and is fearless. He said: "[Athletes like LeBron are] used to being in front of a large group of people and not knowing how it's going to turn out."

The LeBrons

LeBron starred in *The LeBrons*, a series of ads for his Nike shoes. The ads were short cartoons that featured the pretend LeBron family. Each family member represents a different aspect of LeBron James: Wise LeBron, Business LeBron, Athlete LeBron, and Kid LeBron. LeBron himself does the voice for Business.

Ice Cube has been working with LeBron on a show about his high school experiences.

LeBron has promoted Nike sportswear since he went pro in 2003.

YouTube Sensation

After the success of the ads, a **web series** of *The LeBrons* was shown on YouTube in 2011. The series is set in Akron. Kid LeBron is the star and deals with daily challenges. The show tries to send positive messages to kids about issues such as teamwork, family, friendship, and staying in school.

Coming Soon...

A portion of the money earned from the web series went to buying computers for the Boys and Girls Club of America. The next step is to create a full-length animated television show. Someday, you just may see *The LeBrons* on TV.

Long Live the King

It's hard to say what the future holds for LeBron James. He still has many years ahead of him as a basketball player. He hasn't won as many championships as other superstar players, but he's sure to win more either with the Miami Heat or with a future team. Although LeBron signed a six-year contract in 2010, an early termination **clause** means that he could potentially leave the Heat in 2014. Some even speculate that he may return to Cleveland.

One thing is for sure whatever happens LeBron will continue to work hard at his career.

LeBron certainly cannot envision his future without basketball being part of his life. In a 2010 interview with Larry King, LeBron suggested that he may one day like to own a basketball team. He also has high hopes for his son, LeBron Jr., who is already showing impressive talent on the court.

He Said It

Win, lose, or draw, I'm playing because I'm grateful that I'm a kid from Akron, Ohio, that made it to the NBA, that made his dream 'come a reality. That's what I'm happy about, so I can't take it for granted.
—LeBron James, in an interview with ESPN's Rachel Nichols, quoted in Brian Windhorst's article "LeBron James: No more Mr. Bad Guy"

Timeline

1984: LeBron is born in Akron, Ohio on December 30.

1999: LeBron joins St. Vincent-St. Mary High School (STVM) in Akron, where he plays football and basketball.

2000: STVM wins the state championship.

2001: LeBron is named Mr. Ohio Basketball—the first sophomore to win. His school wins the state championship again.

2002: LeBron appears on the cover of *Sports Illustrated* magazine.

2003: STVM wins the national championship. LeBron graduates from high school and is drafted by the NBA's Cleveland Cavaliers.

2004: LeBron is named the NBA Rookie of the Year.

2004: LeBron's first son, LeBron Jr., is born on October 6.

2005: LeBron is voted to the NBA All-Star Game for the first time.

2007: LeBron's second son, Bryce, is born on June 14.

2008: Team USA beat Spain to take gold at the Beijing Olympic Games.

2009: LeBron is named the NBA's Most Valuable Player for the first time.

2010: LeBron becomes a free agent and announces his choice to play for the Miami Heat on a TV special called *The Decision* on ESPN.

2011: LeBron proposes to his high school sweetheart, Savannah, on December 31.

2012: LeBron and his Miami Heat teammates win the NBA Championship.

2012: Team USA take gold at the 2012 Olympic Games.

Glossary

camaraderie A strong friendship

cameo role A small part in a movie or TV show, played by a celebrity

clause Part of a legal document

contract A written agreement

documentary A film that charts the history of a person, place, or thing

draft The process through which new players are selected to join teams in a league

dynasty A family whose members rule for a long time or a team whose players win for many years

endorsement A show of support for a person, product, or service, often in exchange for payment

FIBA Short for the International Basketball Federation, the organization that governs and organizes international basketball competitions

free agent A sports player who is not required by contract to stay with his or her team

free throw A one-point shot taken from the free throw line during a stop in the game; it is awarded to a player who has been fouled by a member of the opposing team while trying to score

marketing Selling products or services

philanthropist A person who works to help people and causes by giving large amounts of money

pitch To propose an idea or product

play-offs The series of games in which the top teams in each division of the league compete to be the league champions

prep-to-pro Describes a player who goes straight from high school to a professional team

ritual An action that is done the same way and at a particular time, place, or event

rookie Beginner

season premiere The first episode of a TV show's new season

web series A show that appears on the Internet, rather than being broadcast on television

Find Out More

Books

James, LeBron & Buzz Bissinger. *Shooting Stars.*
  Penguin Press HC, 2009.

Morgan, David Lee Jr. *LeBron James: The Rise
  of a Star.* Gray & Company, 2003.

Websites

The Official Website of LeBron James
www.lebronjames.com
All the latest info on LeBron on and off the court

NBA player profile
www.nba.com/playerfile/lebron_james/
Keep up on LeBron's game stats

LeBron James Family Foundation
www.lebronjamesfamilyfoundation.org/
Learn more about how LeBron helps kids in Akron

The LeBrons
www.youtube.com/user/TheLeBrons
Watch the original web series

Facebook

www.facebook.com/LeBron

Twitter

https://twitter.com/KingJames

Index

About the Author

Rachel Stuckey has worked for almost a decade in educational publishing, and now works freelance as an editor, writer, and travel blogger. When she's not enjoying her hometown, she's on the road exploring other people's hometowns. She is currently travelling around the world.